# Tiffany

First published in Great Britain in 1997 by
BROCKHAMPTON PRESS
20 Bloomsbury Street, London WC1B 3QA
a member of the Hodder Headline Group

This series of little gift books was made by Frances Banfield, Penny Clarke, Clive Collins, Jack Cooper,
Nick Diggory, John Dunne, David Goodman, Paul Gregory, Douglas Hall, Lucinda Hawksley, Dicky Howett,
Dennis Hovell, Helen Johnson, C. M. Lee, John Maxwell, Patrick McCreeth, Morse Modaberi, Sonya Newland,
Anne Newman, Terry Price, Mike Seabrook, Nigel Soper, Karen Sullivan, Nick Wells and Matt Weyland.

ISBN 1 86019 554 7
A copy of the CIP data is available from the British Library upon request.

Produced for Brockhampton Press by Flame Tree Publishing,
a part of The Foundry Creative Media Company Limited,
The Long House, Antrobus Road, Chiswick, London W4 5HY.

Printed and bound in Italy by L.E.G.O. Spa.

# CELEBRATION

# *Tiffany*

Selected by Karen Sullivan

BROCKHAMPTON PRESS

Louis Comfort Tiffany (1848–1933), was a US artist and glassmaker. He produced stained glass windows, iridescent glass and lampshades, devoting his life to his twin obsessions, light and colour.

Tiffany had known Thomas Edison, the inventor of the incandescent lamp, and had worked with him on light fittings for the new Lyceum Theatre in New York, the first one to be entirely lit by electricity. The standard-model lamps used the stained glass technique and had a bronze base supporting a leaded-glass shade, which provided an exotic and dim glow rather than a practical illumination.

Glory be to God for dappled things –
For skies of couple-colour as a brindled cow;
For rose-moles all in stipple upon trout that swim;
Fresh-firecoal chestnut-falls; finches' wings;

Gerard Manley Hopkins, *'Pied Beauty'*

Design is not for philosophy – it's for life.

Issey Miyake

The walls, old and weather-stained, covered with
hollyhocks, roses, honeysuckles, and a great apricot
tree; the casements full of geraniums....

Mary Russell Mitford, *Our Village*

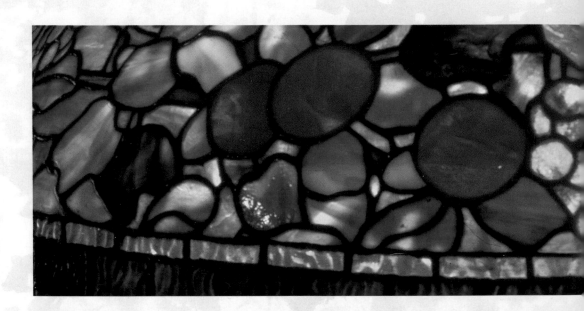

Flowers have spoken to me more than I can tell in
written words. They are the hieroglyphics of angels,
loved by all men for the beauty of their character, though
few can decipher even fragments of their meaning.

Lydia M. Child

Forget the snorting steam and piston stroke,
Forget the spreading of the hideous town;
Think rather of the pack-horse on the down,
And dream of London, small and white and clean,
The clear Thames bordered by its gardens green.

William Morris, *The Earthly Paradise*

Now folds the lily all her sweetness up,
And slips into the bosom of the lake:
So fold thyself, my dearest, thou, and slip
Into my bosom and be lost in me.

Alfred, Lord Tennyson, *'The Princess'*

Art Nouveau was a considered attempt to create a new style in reaction to the academic historicism of the second half of the nineteenth century, instead of imitating and expanding past styles.

Adding copper oxide to clear glass makes blue-green, gold produces red or ruby, cobalt makes blue, manganese oxides yield purple and iron oxide results in various greens.

It is a Pure, Soft, Clear, Steady Light. No smoke, Less Heat…

Advertisement in 1890 for the new incandescent gas mantle

Tiffany resolved the problem of the new electricity's harsh glare by making shades out of coloured glass.

It is not too far-fetched to assume that a rich young American in London [Tiffany] – especially with social connections – and particularly one interested in art – would have met the small circle that included Morris, Rossetti, Burne-Jones, not to mention his compatriot, Whistler.

Mario Amaya

It is curious, is it not, that line and form disappear at a short distance, while colour remains visible at a much longer? It is fairly certain – isn't it? – that the eyes of children at first see only coloured surfaces… colour and movement, not form, are our earliest impressions.

Louis Comfort Tiffany

It lasted a little under two decades, and was influential in creating the next big stylistic entity, Art Deco, but Art Nouveau was very much a flash of brilliance, an eccentric hiccough which captured artistic imaginations at a time when many factions of the arts were disillusioned and jaded.

The water pressed up steadily and noiselessly from the hollow roots and hidden crevices of the plane, forming a wonderful amber pool ere it spilt over the lip of bark on to the earth outside. Mr Lucas tasted it and it was sweet, and when he looked up the black funnel of the trunk he saw sky which was blue, and some leaves which were green....

E. M. Forster, *The Road from Colonus*

I could not make an imposing window with paint.

Louis Comfort Tiffany

I would like to paint as the bird sings.

Claude Monet

Art is man's expression of his joy in labour.

William Morris

Tiffany's lampshade designs were so far superior to any similar product that the term 'Tiffany lamp' came to be a generic term.

A flower – an excellent guide for the decoration of porcelain, furniture, fabrics or costumes. Free and growing out of the earth, or captive in a vase, it presents an artist with the perfect example of the universal creative force – in it he may find form, colour and even expression, a mysterious expression composed of stillness, silence, and the fugitive beauty of things which are born only to die in the same moment. Their frail organisms can be the joy and despair of an artist as much as the most majestic creations of the universe, combining as they do the infinity of a landscape, the beauty of the human face, the sparkle in an eye or the mystery of a smile.

Gustave Geoffroy

Carabin was the creator of the elaborate showcases in the Musée
Galliera which was opened in 1894 to house a permanent collection
of contemporary sculpture and works of art… The director appointed,
Charles Fromentin, was empowered to purchase examples of the
finest craftsmanship of the day and, aided by grants from the
government, collected pottery by Carries, glass by Gallé and Tiffany,
which were accommodated in the vitrines upheld by Carabin's nude
women, considered by some to be unsuitable as they distracted
attention from the objects.

Martin Battersby, *The World of Art Nouveau*

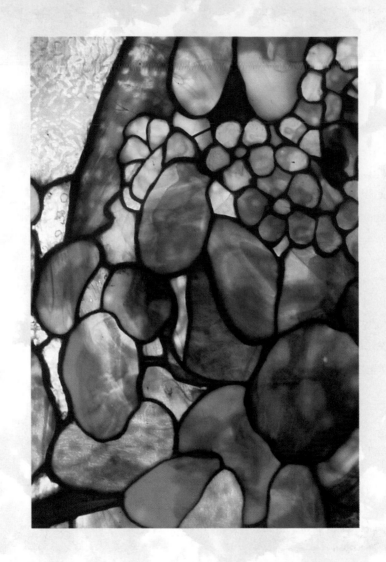

The glistening Iridescence on the vessels of Louis Comfort
Tiffany took a variety of guises… a vase of Cypriot glass,
with gilded drippings streaming down its mottled surface…
abstract leaves set amid streaky tendrils….

*The Art Nouveau Era*

New styles of opalescent glass, new methods of mixing
colours in the glasshouses, have also been tried, and with
many surprising and beautiful results.

*Scribner's Monthly,* 1881

Tiffany's art glass included 'Lustre' ware, 'Agate' ware, 'Cypriote' glass, 'Lava' glass, and 'Paperweight' glass as well as the famous 'Favrile' glass... He used bronze or ceramics for his lamp bases.

The Tiffany lamp is the hearth of the modern household; a central force around which a family may crowd, bathing in the glorious warmth of its light.

*Home Journal,* 1899

The greatest proponent of nature-inspired Art Nouveau in the
United States was Louis Comfort Tiffany, whose creations
included furniture, pottery, metalwork and blown and stained
glass... Unlike many of his French counterparts, notably
Gallé, Tiffany was less concerned with truth to nature than
with technique, texture and dramatic effect.

Jo Marshall

The two essential qualities of glass are its translucence and
its brilliance.

Maurice Marinot, *L'amour de l'Art*

A garden saw I full of blosmy boughs
Upon a river, in a grene mead,
There as sweetness evermore enow is,
With flowers, blue, yellow, and red.

Geoffrey Chaucer, *The Parliament of Fowls*

L'art Nouveau qui est l'image fidèle de l'époque
indécise et vague que nous traversons.

*The Studio*

The world's a garden; pleasures are the flowers,
Of fairest hues, in form and number many:
The lily, first, pure, whitest flower of any,
Rose sweetest rare, with pinked gilliflowers,
The violet, and double marigold,
And pansy too: but after all mischances,
Death's winter comes and kills with sudden cold
Rose, lily, violet, marigold, pink, pansies.

William Shakespeare, *'The Garden'*

What is meant by Art Nouveau?

*The Studio,* 1904

One might have expected that the butterfly would have been a natural accompaniment to the flowers depicted, or used as an element on its own. But it was 'La Libellule', the dragonfly, which for the first time enjoyed a brief spell of popularity as a decorative object… women's heads, torsos and bodies were combined with the iridescent wings of the insect, suitable companions to the 'femmes fleuris' and the flower maidens of Klingsor's magic garden.

Slowly, silently, now the moon
Walks the night in her silver shoon;
This way and that she peers and sees
Silver fruit on silver trees.

Walter de la Mare, *'Silver'*

Four ducks on a pond,
A grass-bank beyond,
A blue sky of spring,
White clouds on the wing.

William Allingham, *'Four Ducks on a Pond'*

I asked the little boy who cannot see,
'And what is colour like?'
'Why, green,' said he,
'Is like the rustle when the wind blows through
The forest; running water, that is blue;
And red is like a trumpet sound; and pink
Is like the smell of roses; and I think
That purple must be like a thunderstorm;
And yellow is like something soft and warm;
And white is a pleasant stillness when you lie
And dream.'

Anonymous

 34

Thou still unravished bride of quietness,
Thou foster-child of silence and slow time,
Sylvan historian, who canst thus express
A flowery tale more sweetly than our thyme:
What leaf-fringed legend haunts about thy shape
Of deities or mortals, or of both,
In Tempe or the dales of Arcady?
What men or gods are these? What maidens loth?
What mad pursuit? What struggle to escape?
What pipes and timbrels? What wild ecstasy?

John Keats, *'Ode on a Grecian Urn'*

My aspens dear, whose airy cages quelled,
Quelled or quenched in leaves the leaping sun,
All felled, felled, are all felled;
Of a fresh and following folded rank
Not spared, not one
That dandled a sandalled
Shadow that swam or sank
On meadow and river and wind-wandering weed-winding bank.

Gerard Manley Hopkins

Art Nouveau is… 'an inspired protest against the absurd survivals from past centuries, which have too long hampered the progress of art… the revolt of intelligence against the tyranny of convention.

*The Studio,* 1904

I have been thinking a great deal about decorative work, and I am going into it as a profession. I believe there is more in it than painting pictures.

Louis Comfort Tiffany

In this land nothing's clear, no colour shape
Except the green. The browns and reds and purples
Change sometimes by the minutes with the moisture
Content of the air, as does the light.

Anthony Cronin, *'Sonnet 15'*


Tree at my window, window tree,
My sash is lowered when night comes on;
But let there never be curtain drawn
Between you and me.

Robert Frost

Imagine the home in which the child, Louis C. Tiffany, found himself. He was not surrounded by the plain, the ugly, or even the simple. His senses were besieged – his hands pressed the curled and ridged handles of French silver cutlery.

Tessa Paul, *The Art of Louis Comfort Tiffany*

I had a chance to travel in the East and to paint where the people, and the buildings also, are clad in beautiful hues, so the pre-eminence of colour was brought forcibly to my attention.

Louis Comfort Tiffany

 42

One impulse from a vernal wood
May teach you more of man,
Of moral evil and of good,
Than all the ages can.

William Wordsworth


O suns and skies and clouds of June,
And flowers of June together,
Ye cannot rival for one hour
October's bright blue weather.

Helen Hunt Jackson

Just as trees and herbs burgeon and flourish in May, the lusty heart that beats in every lover springs, burgeons, buds and flourishes in lusty deeds. For the lusty month of May gives all lovers courage, and constrains them to do things they would not do in any other month. For then all the herbs and trees renew a man and woman, and in like wise lovers call to mind earlier gentleness and earlier service, and many kind deeds forgotten by negligence.

Sir Thomas Malory, *Le Morte d'Arthur*

Mere colour, unspoiled by meaning, and unallied with definite form, can speak to the soul in a thousand different ways.

Oscar Wilde

The lake looked to me, I knew not why, dull and melancholy, and the weltering on the shores seemed a heavy sound. I walked as long as I could amongst the stones of the shore. The wood rich in flowers; a beautiful yellow, palish flower, that looked thick, round, and double, and smelt very sweet – I supposed it was a ranunculus. Crowfoot, the grassy-leaved rabbit-toothed white flower, strawberries, geranium, scentless violets, anemones two kinds, orchids, primroses. The heckberry very beautiful, the crab coming out as a low shrub. Met a blind man, driving a very large beautiful Bull, and a caw – he walked with two sticks. Came home by Clappersgate. The valley very green; many sweet views up to Rydale head....

Dorothy Wordsworth's journal, 14 May 1800

Night is a dead monotonous period under a roof; but in the open world it passes lightly, with its stars and dews and perfumes, and the hours are marked by changes in the face of Nature. What seems a kind of temporal death to people choked between walls and curtains, is only a light and living slumber to the man who sleeps afield.

Robert Louis Stevenson

Lovely rainbow light falling everywhere from the coloured glazing of the skylight.

Mark Twain

Then Sir Launcelot took his sword in his hand and stole to the place where he had spied a ladder beforehand, and that he took under his arm, and carried it through the garden and set it up to the window. And soon the Queen was there ready to meet him....

'I wish,' said the Queen, 'I wish as much as you that you might come in to me.'

'Do you wish, madam,' said Sir Launcelot, 'with your heart that I were with you?'

'Yes, truly,' said the Queen.

'Then I shall prove my might,' said Sir Launcelot, 'for your love.'

And then he laid his hands on the bars of iron and pulled at them with such might that he ripped them right out of the stone walls. And one of the bars cut through the flesh of his hands to the bone. And then he leaped into the chamber to the Queen.

Sir Thomas Malory, *Le Morte d'Arthur*

The purest and most thoughtful minds are those which love colour the most.

John Ruskin

The designers of the Art Nouveau were almost without exception preoccupied with femininity and the objects they designed were invariably created for use by women in boudoirs and salons.

The 'light' room [of Tiffany's 'chapel of art', designed for the 1893 World Columbian Exposition in Chicago] was hung with a chandelier of mother-of-pearl, whose light was reflected in silver and opal-coloured mosaic work. The 'dark' room was green and shifted in tone from a pale leaf-green to the navy-green of deep seawater.

Tessa Paul, *The Art of Louis Comfort Tiffany*


White… is not a mere absence of colour; it is a shining and affirmative thing, as fierce as red, as definite as black… God paints in many colours; but He never paints so gorgeously, I had almost said so gaudily, as when He paints in white.

G. K. Chesterton

True solitude is a din of birdsong, seething leaves, whirling colours, or a clamour of tracks in the snow.

Edward Hoagland

Tiffany said of flowers: 'Their form is distinctly a secondary consideration which comes after the satisfaction we feel in their colour.'

The stippling of a bird's feather, the roughness of bark, the gleam of water, all are reproduced in the great pictorial windows he created.

Tessa Paul, *The Art of Louis Comfort Tiffany*

Happier of happy though I be, like them
I cannot take possession of the sky,
Mount with a thoughtless impulse, and wheel there,
One of a mighty multitude whose way
And motion is a harmony and dance
Magnificent.

William Wordsworth

Luxe, Calme, et Volupté.

A description of Art Nouveau

Flowers… that are so pathetic in their beauty, frail as the clouds, and in their colouring as gorgeous as the heavens, had through thousands of years been the heritage of children – honoured as the jewellery of God only by them – when suddenly the voice of Christianity, counter-signing the voice of infancy, raised them to a grandeur transcending the Hebrew throne, although founded by God himself, and pronounced Solomon in all his glory not to be arrayed like one of these.

Thomas De Quincey


No human being, however great, or powerful, was ever so free as a fish.

John Ruskin

There is a language wrote on earth and sky
By God's own pen in silent majesty;
There is a voice that's heard and felt and seen
In spring's young shades and summer's endless green;
There is a book of poesy and spells
In which that voice in sunny splendour dwells;
There is a page in which that voice aloud
Speaks music to the few and not the crowd;
Though no romantic scenes my feet have trod,
The voice of nature as the voice of God
Appeals to me in every tree and flower,
Breathing his glory, magnitude and power.

John Clare, *'The Voice of Nature'*

I've watched you now a full half-hour,
Self-poised upon that yellow flower;
And, little Butterfly! indeed
I know not if you sleep or feed.
How motionless! and then
What joy awaits you, when the breeze
Hath found you out among the trees,
And calls you forth again!

William Wordsworth, *'To a Butterfly'*

Coloured glass is very pretty and delicate.

Emily, 5

'Tis the last rose of summer,
Left blooming alone;
All her lovely companions are faded and gone.

Thomas Moore

Summer set lip to earth's bosom bare
And left the flushed print in a poppy there.

Francis Thompson

'YES,' I answered you last night,
'No,' this morning, Sir, I say.
Colours seen by candle-light,
Will not look the same by day.

Elizabeth Barrett Browning

The butterfly's attractiveness derives not only from colours and symmetry: deeper motives contribute to it. We would not think them so beautiful if they did not fly, or if they flew straight and briskly like bees, or if they stung, or above all if they did not enact the perturbing mystery of metamorphosis: the latter assumes in our eyes the value of a badly decoded message, a symbol, a sign.

Primo Levi

Butterflies… not quite birds, as they were not quite flowers, mysterious and fascinating as are all indeterminate creatures.

Elizabeth Goudge

Mountains are to the rest of the body of the earth, what violent muscular action is to the body of man. The muscles and tendons of its anatomy are, in the mountain, brought out with force and convulsive energy, full of expression, passion and strength.

John Ruskin

A river seems a magic thing. A magic, moving, living part of the very earth itself – for it is from the soil, both from its depth and from its surface, that a river has its beginning.

Laura Gilpin

To see the Summer Sky
Is Poetry, though never in a Book it lie –
True Poems flee –

Emily Dickinson


Each day I live in a glass room
Unless I break it with the thrusting
Of my senses and pass through
The splintered walls to the great landscape.

Mervyn Peake


Tall poplars – human beings of this earth!

Paul Celan

The moon is up, and yet it is not night;
Sunset divides the sky with her; a sea
Of glory streams along the Alpine height
Of blue Friuli's mountains; Heaven is free
From clouds, but of all colours seems to be, –
Melted to one vast Iris of the West, –
Where the day joins the past Eternity.

Lord Byron, *Childe Harold's Pilgrimage*

It is not growing like a tree
In bulk, doth make men better be;
Or standing long an oak, three hundred year,
To fall a log at last, dry, bald and sere:
A lily of a day,
Is fairer far in May,
Although it fall and die that night;
It was the plant and flower of light.
In small proportions we just beauties see;
And in short measures, life may perfect be.


Ben Jonson

Fair pledges of a fruitful tree,
Why do ye fall so fast?
Your date is not so past;
But you may stay yet here a while,
To blush and gently smile;
And go at last.

Robert Herrick, *'Blossoms'*

I was born upon thy bank, river,
My blood flows in thy stream,
And thou meanderest forever
At the bottom of my dream.

Henry David Thoreau

A lake is the landscape's most beautiful and expressive feature.
It is earth's eye; looking into which the beholder measures
the depth of his own nature.

Henry David Thoreau

Trees, where you sit, shall crowd into a shade:
Where'er you tread, the blushing flow'rs shall rise,
And all things flourish where you turn your eyes.

Alexander Pope

In the Spring, a fuller crimson comes upon the robin's breast,
In the Spring the wanton lapwing gets himself another crest;
In the Spring a livelier iris changes on the burnished dove;
In the Spring a young man's fancy, lightly turns to thoughts of love.

Alfred, Lord Tennyson, *'Locksley Hall'*

Louis Comfort Tiffany was a child – and father – of Art Nouveau.

Tessa Paul, *The Art of Louis Comfort Tiffany*

The face of the water, in time, became a wonderful book – a book that was a dead language to the uneducated passenger, but which told its mind to me without reserve, delivering its most cherished secrets as clearly as if it uttered them with a voice. And it was not a book to be read once and thrown aside, for it had a new story to tell every day.

Mark Twain

Art Nouveau was a style rather than a movement, and like Art Deco it brought together a variety of influences and ideologies to create an artistic umbrella under which many artists and art forms fell. No particular artist or architect represented the school, each interpreting its rather broad assertions in his own way.

A Christmas frost had come at midsummer; a white December storm
had whirled over June; ice glazed the ripe apples, drifts crushed the
blowing roses; on hay-field and corn-field lay a frozen shroud: lanes
which last night blushed full of flowers, today were pathless with
untrodden snow; and the woods which twelve hours since waved leafy
and fragrant as groves between the tropics, now spread, waste, wild
and white as pine-forests in wintry Norway.

Charlotte Brontë, *Jane Eyre*

I believe a leaf of grass is no less than the journey-work of the stars.

Walt Whitman

Notes on Illustrations

**Page 1** Detail of *Leaded Glass Landscape Window, Depicting a Mid-Eastern Vista of an Arab Village* by Tiffany (Burt Sugarman Collection). Courtesy of Christie's Images. **Page 3** *Lotus Leaded Glass and Bronze Table Lamp* by Tiffany (Burt Sugarman Collection). Courtesy of Christie's Images. **Pages 4-5** Detail of *Fruit Leaded Glass and Bronze Table Lamp* by Tiffany (Burt Sugarman Collection). Courtesy of Christie's Images. **Page 6** *"Turtle-Back" Desk Lamp* by Tiffany Studios. Courtesy of Christie's Images. **Page 9** *Landscape (Detail) Flowers and Sky, Leaded Glass Window* by Tiffany (Corning Museum of Glass, New York). Courtesy of Visual Arts Library. **Page 10** *Peony Border Leaded Glass and Bronze Floor Lamp* by Tiffany (Burt Sugarman Collection). Courtesy of Christie's Images. **Page 13** *Dragonfly Leaded Glass and Bronze Table Lamp* by Tiffany (Burt Sugarman Collection). Courtesy of Christie's Images. **Page 14** *Leaded Glass and Bronze "Poppy" Table Lamp* by Tiffany Studios. Courtesy of Christie's Images. **Page 17** *Tiffany Studios Bronze and Glass Filigree Table Lamp* by Tiffany. Courtesy of Christie's Images. **Page 20** *Landscape (Detail) Flowers, Leaded Glass Window* by Tiffany (Corning Museum of Glass, New York). Courtesy of Visual Arts Library. **Page 23** *"Acorn" Leaded Glass and Bronze Table Lamp* by Tiffany Studios. Courtesy of Christie's Images. **Page 24** *Apple Blossom Leaded Glass and Bronze Table Lamp* by Tiffany (Burt Sugarman Collection). Courtesy of Christie's Images. **Page 27** *Begonia Leaded Glass and Bronze Table Lamp* by Tiffany (Burt Sugarman Collection). Courtesy of Christie's Images. **Page 28** *Experimental Gold Favrile Glass Dish with Internal Cypriote Decor* by Tiffany (Burt Sugarman Collection). Courtesy of Christie's Images. **Page 31** *Leaded Glass Landscape Window, Corona Long Island* by Tiffany (Corning Museum of Glass, New York). Courtesy of Visual Arts Library. **Page 32** *Tiffany Favrile Glass Jack-in-the-Pulpit Vase* by Tiffany Studios. Courtesy of Christie's Images. **Page 37** *"Zinnia" Leaded Glass, Mosaic Favrile Glass and Bronze Table Lamp* by Tiffany (Burt Sugarman Collection). Courtesy of Christie's Images. **Page 38** *Eighteen-Light Lily Gilt-Bronze and Favrile Glass Table Lamp* by Tiffany (Burt Sugarman Collection). Courtesy of Christie's Images. **Page 41** *Bronze and Leaded Glass Table Lamp* by Tiffany Studios. Courtesy of Christie's Images. **Page 43** *Rose Bush Leaded Glass Lampshade on a Bronze and Turtle-Back Tile Table Base* by Tiffany (Burt Sugarman Collection). Courtesy of Christie's Images. **Page 44** *Enamel-on-Copper Vase* by Tiffany (Burt Sugarman Collection). Courtesy of Christie's Images. **Page 47** *Leaded Glass Landscape Window depicting a View of Red Flowers and a Stream Flanked* by Tiffany. Courtesy of Christie's Images. **Page 50** *Bronze and Leaded Glass Daffodil Lamp* by Tiffany Studios. Courtesy of Christie's Images. **Page 52** Detail of *Blue Wisteria Leaded Glass and Bronze Table Lamp* by Tiffany (Burt Sugarman Collection). Courtesy of Christie's Images. **Page 55** Detail of

Shade of *Peony Border Leaded Glass and Bronze Floor Lamp* by Tiffany (Burt Sugarman Collection). Courtesy of Christie's Images. **Page 56** *Favrile Glass and Bronze Counter Balance Lamp* by Tiffany Studios. Courtesy of Christie's Images. **Page 59** Detail of *Oriental Poppy Leaded Glass and Bronze Floor Lamp* by Tiffany (Burt Sugarman Collection). Courtesy of Christie's Images. **Page 60** *"Tulip" Leaded Glass and Bronze Table Lamp* by Tiffany Studios. Courtesy of Christie's Images. **Page 65** *Landscape (Detail) Flowers and Sky Leaded Glass Window* by Tiffany (Corning Museum of Glass, New York). Courtesy of Visual Arts Library. **Page 66** *Enamel-on-Copper Cabinet Vase* by Tiffany (Burt Sugarman Collection). Courtesy of Christie's Images. **Page 69** *"Lotus" Leaded Glass and Bronze Table Lamp* by Tiffany. Courtesy of Christie's Images. **Page 70** *Landscape Leaded Glass Window* by Tiffany (Corning Museum of Glass, New York). Courtesy of Visual Arts Library. **Page 75** Detail of *Leaded Glass Landscape Window, Depicting a Mid-Eastern Vista of an Arab Village* by Tiffany (Burt Sugarman Collection). Courtesy of Christie's Images. **Page 77** Detail of *Begonia Leaded Glass and Bronze Table Lamp* by Tiffany (Burt Sugarman Collection). Courtesy of Christie's Images. **Page 78** *"Zinnia" Leaded Glass, Mosaic Favrile Glass and Bronze Table Lamp* by Tiffany (Burt Sugarman Collection). Courtesy of Christie's Images. **Page 81** *Poppy Leaded Glass and Bronze Table Lamp* by Tiffany (Burt Sugarman Collection). Courtesy of Christie's Images. **Page 83** *Blue Wisteria Leaded Glass and Bronze Table Lamp* by Tiffany (Burt Sugarman Collection). Courtesy of Christie's Images.

Acknowledgements: The Publishers wish to thank everyone who gave permission to reproduce the quotes in this book. Every effort has been made to contact the copyright holders, but in the event that an oversight has occurred, the publishers would be delighted to rectify any omissions in future editions of this book. Children's quotes printed courtesy of Herne Hill School; Walter de la Mare reprinted courtesy of the Literary Trustees of Walter de la Mare and the Society of Authors as their agent; Tessa Paul, *The Art of Louis Comfort Tiffany* reprinted courtesy of Grange Books; Robert Frost reprinted from *The Poetry of Robert Frost,* by permission of Jonathan Cape and the Estate of Robert Frost, and Peter A. Gilbert, North Hampshire, USA; Issey Miyake quoted in the *International Herald Tribune,* Paris; *The World of Art Nouveau* reprinted courtesy of Arlington Books.